The Wit and Wisdom of
BENJAMIN FRANKLIN

50 OF HIS MOST BRILLIANT QUOTES AND WHAT THEY MEAN TODAY

By Tony Peters

Published by

T P PUBLICATIONS

4 Pegamoid Road, London

N18 2NG

First edition. August 1, 2023

Copyright © 2023 Tony Peters

ISBN: 978-1-874332-77-0

Table of Contents

Preface

In the annals of history, there are few figures whose legacy shines as brightly as Benjamin Franklin's. A polymath, statesman, inventor, and philosopher, Franklin's influence traverses diverse fields. But it is his timeless quotes and sayings that have etched an indelible mark on the hearts and minds of countless individuals across the globe. From every corner of the world and across the ages, his words have transcended time and cultural boundaries, offering invaluable insights, wisdom, and guidance to people from all walks of life.

My encounter with Benjamin Franklin's story began during my Secondary School days when we delved into 'world history'. Amid the sea of historical information, one name stood out — Benjamin Franklin, one of America's founding fathers. Back then, I hardly grasped the significance of his contributions. However, years later, driven by curiosity, I immersed myself in his life's narrative and was astonished by what I discovered.

Franklin's ability to distill complex ideas into simple, impactful phrases left me in awe. To my surprise, I realised that I had unknowingly incorporated some of his quotes into my conversations and discussions, unaware of their origin. His words, it seemed, had subtly woven themselves into the fabric of my thoughts and expressions.

In this booklet, I humbly share with you a glimpse of the treasures I have gained from delving into the mind of this 18th-century intellectual sage. Here, I offer a selection of his most profound and insightful quotes. It is my sincere hope that these words, born out of love and admiration, will prove not only educational and informative, but also deeply inspirational.

Through the wit and wisdom of Benjamin Franklin, we embark on a journey that transcends time, reminding us that the human potential knows no bounds and that wisdom, regardless of its origin, finds a universal home in our hearts and souls. Join me as we explore the thoughts of this exceptional thinker, and may his words continue to resonate and inspire us all, just as they have for generations before us.

So let the journey begin!

Chapter 1

The Man and His Mission

Benjamin Franklin was one of the Founding Fathers of the United States. He was born on January 17, 1706, in Boston, Massachusetts. He was the 15th of 17 children born to Josiah Franklin, a soap maker, and his wife Abiah Folger.

Despite being born into a modest family, Franklin went on to become one of the most accomplished individuals in the history of America. Here is a brief history of the man and some of his many achievements.

Education:

Franklin attended Boston Latin School but left formal education at the age of 10 to work alongside his father. However, he continued to educate himself through voracious reading and self-study throughout his life.

Apprenticeship:

At the age of 12, Franklin became an apprentice to his older brother James, who was a printer. This marked the beginning of his lifelong association with the printing trade.

Writer and Publisher:

Franklin published his first work, the humorous "A Dissertation upon Liberty and Necessity, Pleasure and Pain," at the age of 17. He went on to publish the Pennsylvania Gazette, which became one of the most influential newspapers in the American colonies.

Founding Father:

Franklin played a crucial role in the American Revolution and the formation of the United States. He was a signer of the Declaration of Independence, representing Pennsylvania, and was involved in drafting the U.S. Constitution.

Public Library:

Franklin founded the first subscription library in America, the Library Company of Philadelphia, in 1731. It was the precursor to public libraries and helped foster a culture of learning.

Firefighting:

In 1736, Franklin organised the Union Fire Company, the first volunteer firefighting company in Philadelphia. He also introduced improved firefighting techniques, such as fire insurance and fire hydrants.

Civic Activism:

Franklin played an active role in public affairs and was known for his civic engagement. He initiated various civic improvement projects, including paving and cleaning the streets, installing street lamps, and establishing a police force.

Poor Richard's Almanack:

Under the pseudonym Richard Saunders, Franklin published Poor Richard's Almanack from 1732 to 1758. It contained practical advice, witty sayings, and weather forecasts and became widely popular, establishing Franklin as a prominent writer.

Electricity and Lightning Rod:

Franklin conducted groundbreaking experiments in electricity and invented the lightning rod. His experiments with flying a kite during a thunderstorm led to his understanding of the nature of electricity and its practical applications.

Franklin Stove:

Franklin invented the efficient wood-burning stove, known as the Franklin stove, in 1741. It provided more heat while consuming less fuel and helped improve home heating in America.

Postal Service:

Franklin created the American postal system in 1753. As the Deputy Postmaster General for the American colonies, Franklin greatly improved the efficiency and reliability of the postal system. He established regular mail service between the colonies and initiated other reforms to make it more accessible.

Diplomat:

Franklin served as a diplomat for the newly formed United States. He played a vital role in securing French support during the American Revolution and negotiated the Treaty of Paris in 1783, which ended the war and recognised American independence.

The Albany Plan of Union:

In 1754, Franklin proposed the Albany Plan of Union, which aimed to create a unified government for the American colonies. Although the plan was not implemented, it laid the groundwork for future discussions on colonial unity.

Scientific Contributions:

Franklin made significant contributions to various scientific fields. He conducted experiments on the nature of electricity, developed theories on heat transfer, and discovered the Gulf Stream, which revolutionised transatlantic travel.

University of Pennsylvania:

Franklin played a pivotal role in establishing the University of Pennsylvania. He helped draft its charter, influenced its curriculum, and served as the university's first president of the board of trustees.

Abolitionism:

Franklin became an outspoken advocate against slavery and became the president of the Pennsylvania Society for

Promoting the Abolition of Slavery. He also published antislavery writings in his newspaper and worked towards the eventual abolition of slavery.

Bifocal Glasses:

Franklin invented bifocal glasses, which allowed individuals with both near and farsightedness to see clearly. His invention greatly improved the quality of life for many people with visual impairments.

Founding Father of the American Philosophical Society:

Franklin co-founded the American Philosophical Society in 1743, which aimed to promote scientific inquiry and intellectual exchange. The society continues to thrive today.

Political Cartoonist:

Franklin was known for his satirical political cartoons, which he used to convey political messages. His iconic "Join, or Die" cartoon, depicting a disjointed snake representing the colonies, became a symbol of colonial unity.

Legacy:

Benjamin Franklin's contributions as an intellectual sage, inventor, writer, and statesman continue to inspire generations. His emphasis on education, civic engagement, scientific inquiry, and moral virtues left a lasting impact on the development of American society.

Benjamin Franklin also wrote his famous autobiography, which remains a classic and provides valuable insights into his life, achievements, and philosophy. His life was a testament to his intellectual curiosity, inventive spirit, and dedication to public service.

Benjamin Franklin passed away on April 17, 1790, in Philadelphia, Pennsylvania, at the age of 84. His life and achievements have made an indelible mark on American history and continue to be celebrated and studied to this day.

Personal Reflection Questions:

- What does Franklin's life and legacy tell you about the vast potential of human beings?

- Do you believe that you can achieve more than you are presently achieving?

- Someone once said, "To do more, you most become more". Who do you need to become and how can you become this person that achieves more?

Chapter 2

Franklin's Personal Philosophy

In order to understand Benjamin Franklin and the things he said and did, we need to understand that he had a well-defined personal philosophy of life. He was strong on self-improvement, industry, practicality, and moral virtues.

He believed in living a purposeful and meaningful life, constantly striving for personal development and contributing to the betterment of society. His personal philosophy can be best summarised by his famous list of thirteen virtues, which he outlined in his autobiography. These virtues served as guiding principles for his conduct and character.

They are:

1. **Temperance:** Avoiding excess and practicing moderation in all aspects of life.

2. **Silence:** Speaking only when necessary and avoiding idle or unnecessary chatter.

3. **Order:** Maintaining order and organisation in one's thoughts, actions, and surroundings.

4. **Resolution:** Having the determination and perseverance to achieve one's goals.

5. **Frugality:** Practicing thrift, avoiding wastefulness, and being wise with money and resources.

6. **Industry:** Being diligent and hardworking in one's pursuits.

7. **Sincerity:** Being genuine, honest, and transparent in interactions with others.

8. **Justice:** Acting with fairness, treating others with respect and equity.

9. **Moderation:** Avoiding extremes and finding balance in all aspects of life.

10. **Cleanliness:** Maintaining personal hygiene and cleanliness in one's surroundings.

11. **Tranquility:** Cultivating inner peace, composure, and tranquility of mind.

12. **Chastity:** Exercising self-control and moderation in matters of sexual conduct.

13. **Humility:** Being modest, acknowledging one's limitations, and valuing other people's contributions.

Franklin believed that by consciously embracing these values and practicing these virtues, we could all lead a morally upright and successful life. He also stressed the importance of constant self-reflection, self-discipline, and personal accountability in adhering to these principles.

Furthermore, Franklin promoted the idea of civic engagement and the pursuit of the greater good. He believed in the power of community, cooperation, and social responsibility. His philosophy encompassed the notion that individuals should strive to make meaningful contributions to society, to be actively involved in public affairs, and to work towards the betterment of their community.

Overall, Benjamin Franklin's personal philosophy emphasised self-discipline, industry, moral virtues, and the pursuit of knowledge and social progress. His principles continue to inspire us today, serving as a timeless guide for personal and societal growth.

Personal Reflection Questions:

- Which of these 13 guiding principles will you say are very important to how you live your life?

- Which ones would you like to add to your life from today?

- What are you willing to do to make it happen sooner than later?

- Start the process and tell someone what you've decided to do. Ask if they can be your accountability partner. Bon voyage!

What to Expect in the Rest of this Book

In the next 5 chapters, we are going to dissect and explain 50 inspirational and educational quotes from Benjamin Franklin. The goal is to understand what they mean, what we can learn from them, and how we can apply them to our lives today.

If any of these quotes don't relate to your circumstances or life demands at this time, just move on to the next one. However, as you grow and experience more, you would want to return to these chapters again and again, for fresh inspiration.

Chapter 3

How Witty?

#1

"By failing to prepare, you are preparing to fail."

The quote "By failing to prepare, you are preparing to fail" holds significant relevance in our lives today. In the modern world, where challenges and opportunities abound, this quote serves as a powerful reminder of the crucial role preparation plays in achieving success. To better understand the meaning of this quote, let's consider a relevant example.

Imagine a professional athlete named Alex who is preparing for an important championship race. Alex understands the significance of proper training, conditioning, and mental preparation to perform at his best. However, due to overconfidence, Alex decides to skip several training sessions and neglects to analyse his competitors' strategies and strengths.

On the day of the race, Alex steps onto the track feeling ill-prepared. As the competition begins, he quickly realises that his physical endurance is lacking, and he struggle to maintain the required pace. Additionally, he is caught off guard by the unexpected tactics employed by his opponents.

Despite his natural talent, his lack of preparation becomes apparent, and he fails to perform up to his potential. In this example, the quote by Benjamin Franklin rings true. Alex's failure to adequately prepare put him at a significant disadvantage. He underestimated the importance of preparation, and paid the price during the race.

The quote emphasises that preparation is not simply an optional step but a crucial foundation for success. It highlights the need to invest time, effort, and resources in honing the necessary skills, gathering knowledge, and understanding the variables at play.

Proper preparation equips you with the tools and confidence required to navigate challenges, make informed decisions, and perform optimally when it matters most. By neglecting the preparation stage, you are essentially setting yourself up for failure.

In Summary:

This quote serves as a reminder to approach any endeavour with a diligent and proactive mindset, recognising that preparation is a key ingredient in the recipe for achievement.

"An investment in knowledge always pays the best interest."

This quote by Benjamin Franklin, suggests that allocating resources, time, and effort towards acquiring knowledge and education yields the greatest returns or benefits. In other words, it emphasises the value and advantages of investing in one's intellectual growth and learning. To illustrate the meaning of this quote, let's consider an example.

Emily is a young professional starting her own business. She recognises the importance of staying up-to-date with industry trends, acquiring new skills, and understanding market dynamics. Instead of solely focusing on short-term gains, Emily decides to invest in her knowledge by attending business workshops, reading industry publications, and engaging in online courses related to entrepreneurship.

As Emily diligently immerses herself in learning, she begins to reap the rewards of her investment. Her expanded knowledge enables her to identify emerging opportunities, make informed decisions, and develop innovative strategies for her business. She applies her newfound expertise to optimise her operations and adapt to changing market conditions.

Over time, Emily's investment in knowledge translates into tangible benefits for her business. She outperforms competitors and attracts a loyal customer base. By staying well-informed and continuously learning, Emily is able to anticipate challenges, seize opportunities, and navigate her business toward long-term success.

In this example, Emily's investment in knowledge pays off handsomely. The knowledge she acquires serves as a valuable asset that enhances her decision-making capabilities, provides a competitive edge, and ultimately leads to the prosperity of her business. While financial investments may fluctuate, knowledge is a form of investment that consistently generates favourable outcomes.

It equips individuals with the tools to navigate complexities, overcome obstacles, and make intelligent decisions in life.

In Summary:

Franklin's quote encourages individuals to recognise the immense power of knowledge and highlights the need to continuously invest in lifelong learning. By investing in knowledge, you can unlock your full potential, make informed decisions, and lead a more fulfilling and successful life.

#3

"Energy and persistence conquer all things."

This quote by Benjamin Franklin emphasises the power and effectiveness of two key qualities: energy and persistence. Let's consider an example to illustrate its meaning.

Imagine a person named Toby who aspires to become a successful author. Toby has a great passion for writing and a vision of publishing a bestselling novel. However, he faces numerous challenges along the way. The publishing industry is competitive, and rejection is a common occurrence. Despite these obstacles, Toby embodies the qualities mentioned in Franklin's quote.

Energy refers to the enthusiasm, dedication, and drive that he brings to the pursuit of his goal. He devotes substantial time and effort to improving his writing skills, researching the publishing industry, and staying up-to-date with literary trends. He attends writing workshops, networks with other authors, and constantly seeks feedback to refine his craft.

Persistence, on the other hand, represents Toby's unwavering determination to overcome setbacks and keep moving forward. Despite receiving multiple rejection letters from publishers, facing self-doubt, and experiencing creative blocks, Toby remains steadfast in his pursuit of becoming a published author. He refuses to give up and continues submitting his work to different publishing houses, revising his manuscripts, and learning from each rejection.

Over time, with energy and persistence, Toby's efforts begin to bear fruit. He receive an acceptance letter from a reputable publishing company. The novel he worked so hard on becomes a bestseller, earning critical acclaim and a loyal readership. Through his unwavering energy and persistence, Toby conquers the challenges and achieves his goal of becoming a successful author.

This example, exemplifies Benjamin Franklin's quote. Toby's energy fuels his pursuit of writing, while his persistence enables him to overcome obstacles and ultimately attain success.

In Summary:

In essence, this quote serves as a reminder that success is not solely determined by inherent talent or luck, but is achieved through a combination of tireless effort, unwavering determination, and a resilient mindset. By staying strong and persistent, we can overcome obstacles, accomplish our goals, and achieve greatness in various areas of life.

#4

"Tell me and I forget, teach me and I may remember, involve me and I learn."

Benjamin Franklin's quote, emphasises the importance of active engagement and hands-on learning experiences. It suggests that true learning occurs when we are actively involved and participate in the learning process. To understand the meaning of this quote, let's consider this example.

Imagine a student named Yemi who is studying chemistry. Her teacher follows a traditional lecture-style approach, delivering information by simply telling the students about different chemical reactions, formulas, and concepts. Although Yemi takes notes during the lectures, she struggles to retain the information and often forgets important details.

In contrast, another teacher takes a different approach. They incorporate interactive experiments, group discussions, and problem-solving activities into their teaching methods. During these sessions, Yemi actively participates, conducts experiments, collaborates with peers, and applies the knowledge to real-life scenarios.

As a result, Yemi's understanding of chemistry significantly improves. Through hands-on experiences and active involvement, she not only remembers the information but also gains a deeper understanding of the subject. The interactive approach fosters critical thinking, problem-solving skills, and a practical understanding of the concepts, which in turn allow Yemi to learn and retain the knowledge more effectively.

This is what Benjamin Franklin's quote teaches. Simply being told things leads to limited retention. However, when we are actively involved in the learning process, we become engaged, motivated, and more likely to grasp and internalise the material.

In Summary:

The quote encourages educators and learners alike to embrace interactive and participatory approaches to education. It recognises that active involvement, whether through hands-on experiences, discussions, or practical applications, is the key to deep and meaningful learning.

"Justice will not be served until those who are unaffected are as outraged as those who are."

Benjamin Franklin's quote, conveys the importance of collective empathy and active engagement in addressing injustice. It suggests that true justice can only be achieved when individuals who are not directly impacted by an injustice show the same level of concern and take action as those who are directly affected. To understand the meaning of this quote, let's consider this example.

Imagine a Community where racial discrimination is prevalent. Members of a marginalised racial group face systemic bias, unequal treatment, and limited opportunities. Those directly affected by this injustice are rightfully outraged and demand change. However, the majority of the community, who are not directly impacted by racial discrimination, remain indifferent and fail to recognise the severity of the issue.

In this scenario, justice is not fully served. Despite the efforts of the marginalised group, the lack of engagement and empathy from the unaffected majority perpetuates the injustice. It is only when individuals from the unaffected group begin to understand the gravity of the situation, empathise with the affected individuals, and actively join the fight for justice that meaningful progress can be made.

The quote emphasises that achieving justice requires collective action and solidarity. It calls for individuals to move beyond their own self-interests and recognise the importance of equality and fairness for all members of society. The quote serves as a reminder that justice is not an isolated pursuit but a collective responsibility.

It encourages individuals to broaden their perspectives, empathise with other people's experiences, and take action to address and rectify injustice. Only through unified efforts and a shared commitment to justice can society truly progress towards a more equitable and fair future.

In Summary:

When those who are unaffected by an injustice become as outraged as those who are directly impacted, they amplify the voices of the marginalised, mobilise support, and work towards justice and systemic change.

#6

"Never confuse motion with action."

The quote "Never confuse motion with action" by Benjamin Franklin carries a valuable message for us today. In our fast-paced and busy world, the quote serves as a reminder to distinguish between mere busyness or movement and purposeful, productive action.

It is easy today, to fall into the trap of being constantly busy and engaged in various activities or tasks, but not necessarily making meaningful progress. Franklin's quote cautions against this by highlighting the importance of discerning between motion (which implies activity without a clear purpose or impact) and action (which signifies deliberate and effective steps towards a desired goal).

In our personal and professional lives, it is essential to focus on actions that align with our goals and values. Simply being busy or engaged in constant activity does not guarantee progress or success. Instead, the quote encourages us to evaluate whether our actions are truly productive and impactful.

To apply this quote in our lives today, we must strive to prioritise quality over quantity, and purpose over busyness. It entails critically assessing the tasks and activities we undertake, ensuring they contribute to our long-term objectives.

By avoiding the trap of confusing motion with action, we can allocate our time and energy more effectively, making tangible progress and achieving desired outcomes.

In Summary:

This quote by Franklin, prompts us to be mindful of how we spend our time and to focus on taking purposeful, meaningful actions that lead us closer to our goals. Engaging in mere motion or superficial busyness is futile and unproductive.

"When you're finished changing, you're finished."

This quote by Benjamin Franklin conveys the idea that personal growth, adaptability, and a willingness to embrace change are vital for ongoing success and fulfilment in life.

Franklin's quote suggests that change is a constant and inevitable part of life. It emphasises the importance of being open to new ideas, perspectives, and experiences. In a rapidly evolving world, individuals who resist change or become complacent in their ways risk stagnation and missed opportunities for growth.

The quote encourages continuous self-improvement and learning. It implies that personal development is an ongoing journey that extends beyond reaching a specific goal or milestone. By remaining open to change, individuals can expand their knowledge, skills, and perspectives, allowing for personal and professional growth.

Moreover, the quote highlights the idea that change brings new possibilities and opportunities. By embracing change, individuals can adapt to new circumstances, overcome challenges, and seize emerging prospects. It emphasises the importance of remaining proactive and agile in the face of changing environments and circumstances.

In Summary:

Benjamin Franklin's quote serves as a reminder that personal growth and adaptability are lifelong pursuits. It encourages us to embrace change, continually seek self-improvement, and remain open to new experiences. By doing so, individuals can navigate the complexities of life, seize new opportunities, and maintain a sense of purpose and fulfilment.

#8

"When you're down to nothing, God is up to something."

The quote by Benjamin Franklin, suggests that even in the most challenging and hopeless situations, we must always believe that God is at work. It implies that when we feel at our lowest and have exhausted all our options, there is still a source of hope, guidance, and assistance available to us.

Imagine if you had a friend called Ravi. Ravi is facing a series of setbacks in his professional and personal life. He loses his job, experiences a financial crisis, and is struggling to keep keep his girl friend happy. He feels overwhelmed and completely helpless, with no clear solution in sight. He feels like he is "down to nothing."

Ravi remembers what he learnt in Sunday School, and turns to his faith. He puts his trust in God again, believing that despite his current struggles, there is a divine plan unfolding. The following month, unexpected opportunities begin to emerge.

Ravi receives a job offer from a company he didn't expect to hear back from, providing him financial stability. Additionally, he connects with a supportive Church Community who help him rebuild his life and find new purpose. Through these positive developments, Ravi realises that despite being at his lowest point, there was a higher plan unfolding for his life.

In this example, Benjamin Franklin's quote becomes evident. When Ravi felt like he had nothing left, God showed him that He had a better plan. It signifies the idea that in our darkest moments, when we are stripped of everything, we can persevere because God is at work in the background.

In Summary:

The quote emphasises the importance of faith, resilience, and trust in times of adversity. It encourages us to remain hopeful, even when faced with seemingly insurmountable challenges, because there is always a bigger Sovereign plan at play.

#9

"Early to bed and early to rise makes a man healthy, wealthy, and wise."

The quote by Benjamin Franklin, "Early to bed and early to rise makes a man healthy, wealthy, and wise," conveys the importance of establishing disciplined sleeping and waking habits. It suggests that by going to bed early and waking up early, individuals can cultivate positive outcomes in various aspects of their lives.

Consider a person named Sarah who struggles with her daily routine. She often stays up late at night, compromising her sleep, and consequently wakes up feeling groggy and lethargic in the morning. Sarah finds it challenging to concentrate during the day, lacks the energy to pursue her goals, and frequently succumbs to unhealthy habits such as skipping breakfast or relying on caffeine.

Recognising the need for change, Sarah decides to adopt Benjamin Franklin's advice. She adjusts her sleep schedule, prioritising going to bed early and waking up early. As a result, Sarah experiences several positive effects.

Firstly, she notices an improvement in her physical and mental well-being. She feels rejuvenated, more energised, alert, and focused throughout the day. Secondly, her productivity increases, leading to positive impacts on her professional and personal life. She has more time in the morning to engage in activities such as exercise, planning her day, and pursuing personal growth. She becomes more organised and her performance at work leads to career advancement and financial stability.

In this example, the quote by Benjamin Franklin resonates. Sarah's commitment to going to bed early and waking up early contributes to her improved health, increased productivity, and her positive career prospects. It exemplifies the benefits of a well-regulated sleep schedule and its positive influence on every area of her life.

In Summary:

The quote serves as a reminder of the importance of establishing healthy sleep habits and the potential rewards that come with it. By prioritising adequate rest and waking up early, we can optimise our physical and mental well-being, enhance our productivity, and grow personally and professionally.

#10

"A small leak will sink a great ship."

This quote by Benjamin Franklin, emphasises the significance of addressing even the smallest problems or issue before they escalate and cause substantial damage. It illustrates that seemingly minor issues, if left unattended, can lead to significant consequences.

Imagine a successful company that prides itself on its impeccable reputation and strong financial position. However, the company's management becomes complacent and fails to address a small operational inefficiency. This inefficiency may be a minor flaw in the supply chain or a small oversight in quality control.

Initially, the impact of the small issue may be negligible, with minimal disruptions or financial losses. However, as time passes, the overlooked problem begins to affect other areas of the business. It leads to delays in product delivery, customer dissatisfaction, and a decline in sales.

The initial small leak has now developed into a significant problem, negatively impacting the company's profitability. Customer stop trusting them too. Despite its previous stability, the company finds itself struggling to stay afloat and recover from the damage caused by the unaddressed issue. The small leak that was initially disregarded eventually sinks the great ship of the company's success.

The quote carries broader implications beyond the business context. It serves as a reminder to us in all aspects of life, to pay attention to the small details, to address minor issues, and to prevent them from escalating into major challenges. Whether in our personal relationships, our health, or our finances, attending to small problems can prevent them from growing into overwhelming difficulties.

In Summary:

Ultimately, this quote encourages proactive and diligent problem-solving. It highlights the need to be vigilant and take swift action when confronted with even the smallest 'leaks' or 'deficiencies' to ensure the long-term stability, success, and well-being of individuals, endeavours, and organisations.

Chapter 4

How True?

#11

"There are no gains without pains."

This quote essentially means that in order to achieve or attain something valuable, one must be willing to put in effort, endure hardships, and face challenges along the way. Success and progress often require hard work, dedication, and perseverance.

To illustrate this concept, let's consider the example of a student preparing for an important exam. Imagine you have a goal of achieving a high score in a challenging subject like mathematics. In order to accomplish this, you'll need to invest time and effort into studying, understanding complex concepts, and practicing problem-solving skills.

At first, you might find the material difficult to grasp, leading to feelings of frustration or confusion. However, by pushing through these initial struggles and persisting in your efforts, you start to make incremental progress.

As the exam date approaches, you notice that your hard work is paying off. You begin to understand the subject more deeply, your problem-solving abilities improve, and your confidence grows. On the day of the exam, you feel well-prepared and perform exceptionally well, achieving the high score you aimed for.

In this example, the quote by Benjamin Franklin becomes evident. The gains in the form of a high score on the exam were only possible because you were willing to endure the pains of studying, facing challenging concepts, and overcoming initial difficulties. Without putting in the effort and embracing the hardships, the desired outcome would not have been achievable.

In Summary:

This quote by Benjamin Franklin serves as a reminder that success, growth, and achievement require effort, perseverance, and a willingness to face and overcome obstacles. It encourages us to embrace the challenges that come with pursuing our goals, understanding that the rewards we seek are often a result of the hard work and determination we put into our endeavours.

#12

"The best way to predict the future is to create it."

This quote conveys the idea that we have the power to shape our own future through proactive actions and intentional decision-making. Instead of merely waiting for things to happen or relying on predictions, we can take charge of our lives and actively work towards the future we desire.

To illustrate this concept, imagine you have a deep interest in environmental sustainability and want to contribute to a greener future. You believe in the potential of renewable energy sources to address climate change and reduce our reliance on fossil fuels. Instead of merely hoping for a cleaner future, you decide to take action and create it.

You start by educating yourself on the various forms of renewable energy, such as solar, wind, and hydroelectric power. You research the latest advancements in the field, studying successful projects and understanding the benefits and challenges associated with each technology.

Armed with knowledge and determination, you begin reaching out to local communities, government officials, and environmental organisations to raise awareness about the importance of renewable energy. You organise community meetings, give presentations, and engage in discussions to curry support for your sustainable initiatives.

Inspired by your vision, you connect with like-minded individuals who share your passion and expertise. Together, you form a team and decide to start a renewable energy company. You go through the process of securing funding, acquiring necessary permits, and identifying suitable locations for your projects.

As your company takes shape, you collaborate with engineers and energy experts to design and implement innovative renewable energy systems. You install solar panels on rooftops, and develop wind farms. Each project not only contributes to a cleaner future but also creates job opportunities and economic growth in the communities you serve.

Over time, your company's impact grows, and you become a leading figure in the renewable energy industry. Your initiatives gain recognition and support on a larger scale. Through your proactive efforts, you not only planned a more sustainable future but actively created it by implementing tangible solutions and inspiring change.

In this example, the quote by Benjamin Franklin is exemplified. Instead of simply hoping for a future with cleaner energy, you took proactive steps to create it. By educating yourself, raising awareness, forming a team, and implementing renewable energy projects, you actively shaped the future you envisioned.

In Summary:

This quote serves as a powerful reminder that we have the ability to turn our visions and aspirations into reality. By taking initiative, pursuing our passions, and actively working towards our goals, we can create a future that aligns with our values and aspirations. It encourages us to be proactive, innovative, and visionary—and reminds us that we have the power to shape a part of the world we wish to live in.

#13

"Lost time is never found again."

This quote highlights the importance of valuing and utilising our time effectively because once time is gone, it cannot be recovered or regained. It emphasises the significance of not wasting or squandering our precious moments as they are finite and irreplaceable.

Imagine you have a passion for playing a musical instrument, let's say the guitar. You've always wanted to learn and become proficient in playing it, but due to various reasons, you keep postponing and neglecting your practice sessions.

Months, and even years go by, and you realise that you haven't dedicated the time and effort needed to develop your guitar skills. The hours you could have spent practicing and honing your technique were instead filled with other activities that didn't contribute to your musical growth.

One day, you attend a concert featuring a talented guitarist who captivates the audience with her skilful playing. As you watch her effortlessly strumming the strings and producing beautiful melodies, you can't help but feel a sense of regret and missed opportunities. You realise that if you had utilised your time more effectively and consistently practiced the guitar, you could have been on a similar path.

However, the time that slipped away without dedicated practice cannot be recovered. The hours, days, and months spent without actively investing in your guitar skills are lost forever. You understand the significance of the quote by Benjamin Franklin, as it resonates with the regret you feel for not making the most of your time to pursue your musical passion, when you had the time.

This quote serves as a powerful reminder to value and prioritise our time wisely. It highlights the importance of taking action, seizing opportunities, and consistently working towards our goals. Lost time cannot be regained, so it urges us to make the most of each moment, ensuring that we allocate time and effort to activities that align with our aspirations.

In Summary:

The quote emphasises the need to prioritise our passions and allocate time to pursue them. It encourages us to avoid procrastination and make consistent progress towards our goals. By doing so, we can avoid the regret of lost opportunities, and instead, make meaningful strides towards achieving mastery in our chosen pursuits. It emphasises the irretrievable nature of time. Because once time is wasted, it cannot be recovered.

"Many people die at twenty-five and aren't buried until they are seventy-five."

This quote speaks to the notion that some individuals live their lives in a state of stagnation, lacking purpose, ambition, and personal growth. They may physically exist, but they fail to truly live—and they allow their dreams and aspirations to wither away over time.

For example, imagine you have a deep passion for a creative field, such as writing, painting, or photography. However, due to societal pressures, fear of failure, or laziness, you choose to pursue a conventional office job that offers stability but doesn't align with your true interests and talents.

Years pass by, and you find yourself going through the motions, merely existing without a sense of purpose or fulfilment. The creative spark within you remains dormant and untapped, as you compromise your passion for the sake of security or societal expectations.

Deep down, you know that you are capable of so much more; and that your true potential lies in pursuing your creative aspirations. However, you allow the fear of change and the comfort of familiarity to hold you back. As a result, you remain stuck in a state of dissatisfaction and regret, burying your dreams and never giving them a chance to flourish.

In this example, the quote by Benjamin Franklin becomes evident. While you may physically be alive and functioning, your true self—the one driven by passion, purpose, and personal growth—feels as though it has died.

This quote serves as a powerful reminder to break free from the chains of conformity and to live a life that is authentic and aligned with our passions. It urges us to seize the present moment, pursue our dreams, and make the most of the time we have.

Rather than succumbing to a life of mediocrity and regret, it encourages us to embrace personal growth, take risks, and nurture our passions, so that we may truly live a life that is meaningful and fulfilling.

In Summary:

I encourage you to reflect on this quote and consider whether you are truly living a life that brings you joy and fulfilment. Embrace your passions, overcome the fear of change, and take steps towards personal growth and self-actualisation. Remember, life is too precious to allow it to pass by without truly living it to the fullest.

#15

"Diligence is the mother of good luck."

This quote suggests that hard work, persistence, and consistent effort are the foundation for creating favourable opportunities and achieving success. It emphasises that 'good old luck' often favours those who demonstrate dedication and unwavering commitment to their goals.

Consider this scenario: You are preparing for a job interview. You have applied for a position at a reputable company that aligns perfectly with your career aspirations. You know that competition is high, and many qualified candidates are vying for the same opportunity.

To improve your chances of success, you diligently research the company, the job role, and the industry. You invest time in understanding the company's values, their mission, and culture. You also study the job requirements and identify how your skills and experiences can benefit the company.

Armed with this knowledge, you prepare for the interview by practicing common interview questions. You also work on improving your presentation skills and your overall professional demeanour. On the day of the interview, you arrive early, dressed appropriately, and showcase confidence and enthusiasm. You engage in thoughtful and well-prepared responses and show them your passion for the role.

The interviewers are impressed by your knowledge, preparation, and genuine interest in the company. And as a result of your diligence, you receive a job offer from the company. Your friends may attribute this success to luck, but you recognise that it was your diligence and enthusiasm that paved the way.

That is what Benjamin Franklin was highlighting in this quote. By diligently preparing for the job interview, you created favourable circumstances and positioned yourself for success. The good luck that came your way was not mere chance, but a result of your hard work and commitment to excellence.

In Summary:

This quote serves as a reminder that success often stems from the diligent and consistent effort we invest in our pursuits. When we take the time to thoroughly prepare, continuously improve our skills, and demonstrate dedication to our goals, we increase the likelihood of encountering fortunate opportunities.

#16

"Either write something worth reading or do something worth writing about."

This quote by Benjamin Franklin, encapsulates the idea that one should strive to engage in meaningful actions or create valuable content that leaves a lasting impact on others. It encourages individuals to pursue projects or goals that are worthy of attention.

The quote suggests that there are two paths to making a meaningful contribution. The first path is to write something worth reading. This refers to the act of creating written works, such as books, articles, or essays, that contain valuable insights, knowledge, or stories. By producing compelling and impactful written content, we can share our perspectives, inspire others, and contribute to the collective wisdom of society.

The second path is to do something worth writing about. This implies engaging in actions or experiences that are noteworthy, memorable, and significant. By actively participating in meaningful endeavours, we can create stories and accomplishments that others find worth recounting or sharing through writing.

In essence, the quote encourages individuals to make a meaningful impact on the world either through their creative works or through their actions. It emphasises the importance of creating value, inspiring people, and leaving a lasting legacy. It suggests that we should strive for significance and strive to make a difference in the lives of others.

For example, let's consider a social activist who is passionate about addressing environmental issues. In addition to writing about the importance of environmental conservation, the activist takes action by organising community clean-up initiatives, advocating for sustainable practices, and raising awareness about the impact of human activities on the planet.

By actively engaging in these efforts, they not only contribute to environmental preservation, but also provide inspiring stories and examples worth writing about, capturing the attention of others and motivating them to take action.

In Summary:

In this quotation Benjamin Franklin emphasises the importance of making a meaningful impact. Engage in activities or create works that are worthy of attention and have a lasting influence.

#17

"Guests, like fish, begin to smell after three days."

This quote by Benjamin Franklin conveys the idea that extended stays or prolonged visits from guests can sometimes lead to discomfort or strain on relationships. It suggests that while hospitality and welcoming guests are important, there can be a point where their presence becomes burdensome or annoying.

In a literal sense, this quote draws a parallel between guests and fish. Just as fish left out for too long can become unpleasant due to its odour, hosting guests for an extended period may lead to similar feelings of discomfort or inconvenience.

In a broader context, this quote can be applied metaphorically to various situations in modern life. It serves as a reminder that there is a balance to be maintained in hosting or accommodating others, whether it's family, friends, or acquaintances. While it is wonderful to extend hospitality, there may come a point when boundaries need to be established to preserve the harmony and well-being of both hosts and guests.

In today's context, this quote may be a gentle way to communicate to guests that their stay has reached a point where it may be causing inconvenience or strain on the host's resources or personal space. By acknowledging the importance of balancing hospitality with personal comfort, the host can set reasonable expectations for the duration of a guest's stay and ensure a more harmonious environment for everyone involved.

However, it's important to approach such situations with tact and sensitivity, as the quote should not be used as an excuse to be inhospitable or unwelcoming. Open communication, setting clear expectations, and discussing any concerns openly and respectfully can help maintain positive relationships and avoid misunderstandings.

In Summary:

Overall, this quote by Benjamin Franklin reminds us to be mindful of the dynamics of hosting guests and to strike a balance between hospitality and personal comfort. It humorously suggests that extended stays can become tiresome, and it serves as a reminder to be considerate and not overstay one's welcome.

#18

"Genius without education is like silver in the mine."

This quote by Benjamin Franklin, suggests that innate talent or brilliance, without proper education and cultivation, remains untapped and under-utilised. It compares the unexplored potential of a gifted individual to silver that is still in the ground, waiting to be mined and transformed into something valuable.

In essence, the quote emphasises the importance of education and learning in harnessing and refining one's natural abilities. It implies that raw talent alone is not enough to achieve true greatness or make a significant impact. Without the necessary knowledge, skills, and guidance that education provides, even the most brilliant individuals may struggle to realise their full potential.

In today's society, access to education and lifelong learning opportunities is more readily available than ever before. The quote serves as a reminder that individuals should actively seek out educational experiences, whether through formal schooling, self-study, mentorship, or practical training, to fully unlock their genius and make a meaningful contribution.

Additionally, this quote can be used to advocate for equal educational opportunities. It emphasises the importance of providing quality education to all individuals, regardless of their race, gender, background or circumstances. It also highlights the idea that talent is present in every corner of society, but without proper education and support, many potential geniuses may go undiscovered or fail to reach their true potential.

It suggests that education is the key to transforming their raw potential into something valuable and impactful.

In Summary:

This quote by Benjamin Franklin conveys the notion that raw talent or genius requires education to be fully realised. It underscores the significance of education in unlocking individual potential, advocating for equal educational opportunities, and inspiring individuals to embrace lifelong learning for personal growth and the betterment of society.

#19

"He that can have patience can have what he will."

This quote emphasises the power of patience. By being patient, you can achieve desired outcomes and overcome challenges with greater ease.

Imagine a person who has a strong desire to start their own business. They have a clear vision, innovative ideas, and a strong entrepreneurial spirit. However, they are aware that building a successful business takes time, effort, and patience.

In this context, the quote suggests that if the aspiring entrepreneur can cultivate patience, they can achieve their entrepreneurial ambitions. Starting a business involves various challenges, including developing a business plan, securing funding, building a customer base, and navigating through setbacks and obstacles.

The aspiring entrepreneur may face moments of uncertainty and setbacks along the way. However, if they maintain patience, they can persevere through these challenges. They understand that building a successful business takes time and that each step forward, even if small, brings them closer to their goals.

With patience, the aspiring entrepreneur can continue to learn, adapt, and refine their business strategy. They take the necessary steps to build a strong foundation, develop relationships, and provide value to their customers. They understand that success does not happen overnight, but through persistent efforts and a long-term perspective.

Over time, with patience and perseverance, the entrepreneur's business begins to grow. They attract customers, establish a positive reputation, and experience the satisfaction of seeing their vision come to life. By having the patience to withstand challenges and remain focused on their goals, they can ultimately achieve the success they envisioned.

In Summary:

Overall, the quote encourages individuals to embrace patience as they pursue their entrepreneurial endeavours, recognising that success often comes to those who persistently pursue their goals with resilience and a long-term perspective.

"The only thing that is more expensive than education is ignorance."

This quote emphasises the importance and value of education while highlighting the negative consequences of ignorance. In this context, "education" refers to the process of acquiring knowledge, skills, and understanding through formal or informal means.

Education can be obtained through various channels such as schools, universities, books, experiences, and interactions with others. It broadens our horizons, enhances our abilities, and equips us with the tools to navigate the world effectively.

On the other hand, "ignorance" refers to a lack of knowledge or awareness about a particular subject. Ignorance can stem from a variety of reasons, including lack of access to education, indifference towards learning, or unwillingness to expand one's knowledge. Benjamin Franklin's quote suggests that while education may have its costs, the consequences of remaining ignorant are far more detrimental and costly.

By emphasising the value of education, Franklin encourages individuals to prioritise learning and self-improvement. He suggests that investing in education is a wise choice because it empowers individuals, enhances their understanding of the world. Ultimately, the quote serves as a reminder that the long-term benefits of education outweigh its initial costs, and it is a worthwhile investment in oneself and one's future.

In Summary:

This quote highlights the high cost of ignorance and the benefits of investing in education. Lack of knowledge can lead to costly mistakes and missed opportunities.

Chapter 5

How Simple?

#21

"Don't put off until tomorrow what you can do today."

The quote "Don't put off until tomorrow what you can do today" encourages individuals to avoid procrastination and to take action promptly instead of delaying tasks or responsibilities. This quote emphasises the importance of time management and productivity.

It suggests that it is more efficient and beneficial to complete tasks, or assignments in a timely manner rather than postponing them. By doing so, we can avoid accumulating a backlog of unfinished work and the stress that comes with it.

Franklin's quote reflects the idea that delaying tasks until the future can lead to wasted opportunities, decreased productivity, and increased stress. Procrastination often results in a last-minute rush to complete tasks, which can compromise the quality of work, or result in missed deadlines. It can also lead to a sense of dissatisfaction, as we may feel overwhelmed by the growing pile of unfinished tasks.

By urging individuals to act today instead of postponing, Franklin highlights the importance of discipline, self-motivation, and efficient time management.

In Summary:

Overall, the quote serves as a reminder to prioritise tasks and make efficient use of time. It encourages us to develop a proactive mindset and avoid the pitfalls of procrastination.

#22

"A penny saved is a penny earned."

Benjamin Franklin's quote highlights the importance of financial prudence, thriftiness, and the long-term value of saving money. In this quote, "a penny saved" refers to the act of preserving and not spending money unnecessarily. Franklin suggests that when you save money rather than spending it, you are essentially increasing your wealth or income.

By emphasising the value of saving, he implies that the money you retain has the same worth as money earned through active income generation. The quote encourages individuals to adopt a mindset of financial responsibility and frugality.

It promotes the idea that even small amounts saved can accumulate over time, leading to significant financial benefits. By being mindful of expenses and finding ways to cut costs, we can improve our financial well-being and create a foundation for future financial security.

Additionally, the quote reflects the idea of resourcefulness and avoiding wastefulness. It encourages us to make thoughtful choices about our spending habits, prioritise our financial goals, and avoid unnecessary expenditures.

In summary:

Franklin emphasises the value of frugality and saving money. It encourages us to recognise the long-term value of every penny saved, as it contributes to our financial stability. By adopting a thrifty mindset and avoiding wastefulness, we can build a stronger financial foundation and achieve our financial goals.

#23

"There are three things extremely hard: steel, a diamond, and to know oneself."

In this statement, Franklin is emphasising the difficulty associated with three distinct things. Firstly, he mentions steel and a diamond. Both steel and diamonds are known for their hardness and durability. By including them in his statement, Franklin is highlighting their physical toughness, indicating that they are challenging to manipulate or break.

Secondly, Franklin brings attention to the task of knowing oneself. This phrase refers to self-awareness and understanding one's own nature, desires, strengths, weaknesses, and motivations. Franklin suggests that gaining this deep understanding of oneself is extremely challenging—to say the least.

By combining these elements, Franklin implies that just as steel and diamonds present formidable physical challenges, comprehending one's own nature, thoughts, tendencies, decisions, and peculiar characteristics is equally arduous.

In Summary:

Franklin suggests that understanding oneself is a difficult task. Self-reflection and self-awareness require deep introspection and exploration.

#24

"It takes many good deeds to build a good reputation, and only one bad one to lose it."

When Benjamin Franklin wrote, "It takes many good deeds to build a good reputation, and only one bad one to lose it," he was expressing the delicate nature of reputation and how it is shaped. Franklin's statement suggests that maintaining a positive reputation requires consistent acts of goodwill and virtuous behaviour over time.

Imagine a renowned chef who has spent years building a stellar reputation through hard work, and consistently providing outstanding dining experiences. Patrons praise the chef's delicious creations and exceptional service, and the chef becomes widely respected in the culinary world.

However, one evening, due to an unfortunate oversight, a diner is served a dish that contains an allergen they specifically mentioned. This mistake leads to a severe allergic reaction, causing harm to the customer. News of this incident spreads quickly, and the chef's reputation takes a significant hit.

Despite years of hard work and countless positive dining experiences, this single instance of negligence causes the chef's reputation to suffer. The media focuses on the incident, customers lose trust, and the chef's previously esteemed image becomes tarnished.

In this example, Benjamin Franklin's quote becomes apparent. The chef's reputation, built over time through numerous good deeds (e.g. creating excellent dishes, delivering remarkable service), crumbles due to one expensive oversight.

In Summary:

The quote serves as a cautionary reminder of how easily a reputation can be damaged, even after extensive efforts to establish it. It emphasises the need to consider the long-term consequences of our actions on our reputation and the significance of building and safeguarding a positive image through sustained virtuous effort.

"Be slow in choosing a friend, but slower in changing him (or her)."

Benjamin Franklin's quote, "Be slow in choosing a friend, but slower in changing him (or her)," offers valuable guidance regarding friendship and the process of selecting and maintaining meaningful relationships.

In this statement, Franklin underscores the importance of taking ample time and care when choosing a friend. He advises against rushing into friendships without thoughtful consideration. By being deliberate in our selection, we can better assess that person's character, values, and compatibility with our own.

Moreover, Franklin goes a step further by emphasising the need to be even slower when it comes to changing or ending a friendship. Once a bond is established, Franklin suggests exercising patience and loyalty. Instead of hastily severing ties, he encourages giving the relationship time and space to evolve, mend any misunderstandings, or address challenges that may arise.

Franklin's wisdom reminds us that true friendships require both discernment and commitment. By being patient in our choices and steadfast in our loyalty, we can foster enduring connections that enrich our lives.

In Summary:

This quote serves as a reminder to approach friendship with prudence, invest in meaningful relationships, and be willing to work through difficulties before considering drastic changes.

#26

"Never ruin an apology with an excuse."

When Benjamin Franklin wrote this idiom, he conveyed a powerful message about the importance of genuine and sincere apologies. Franklin's statement suggests that when we apologise for something, it is crucial not to diminish the impact of our apology by offering excuses or justifications for our actions.

By avoiding excuses in an apology, Franklin implies that taking responsibility for our actions and expressing remorse should be the primary focus. Offering excuses can undermine the sincerity of an apology and diminish its effectiveness in addressing a mistake.

For example: Let's say you accidentally broke a valuable item that belonged to your friend. Recognising your mistake and wanting to make amends, you approach your friend and say, "I'm truly sorry that I broke your item. It was careless of me, and I understand how much it meant to you. I take full responsibility for my actions, and I'm willing to do whatever it takes to make it right."

In this example, you avoid making excuses such as blaming external factors or downplaying your responsibility. Instead, you acknowledge your carelessness, express genuine remorse, and demonstrate your willingness to take appropriate actions to rectify the situation. By refraining from ruining the apology with excuses, you show sincerity and a genuine desire to make amends.

Franklin's idiom reminds us to focus on accountability, empathy, and true remorse when apologising, ensuring that our apologies carry the weight they deserve and contribute to the healing or reconciliation process. If married couples heeded this advice, there would be less pain and conflict in every home.

In Summary:

Apologies should be genuine and not accompanied by excuses. So take full responsibility for your actions and leave it there.

#27

"It is easier to prevent bad habits than to break them."

When Benjamin Franklin wrote, "It is easier to prevent bad habits than to break them," he was emphasising the difficulty of breaking established negative behaviour compared to avoiding them altogether. In this context, Franklin suggested that it is more efficient and effective to proactively avoid developing harmful habits rather than trying to overcome them later.

For example, it is easier to prevent smoking than to quit smoking once you have become addicted to nicotine.

It is easier to prevent procrastination by setting a schedule and sticking to it than to break the habit of procrastination once it has become a part of your routine.

It is easier to prevent overspending by creating a budget and sticking to it than to break the habit of overspending once you have accumulated debt.

It is easier to prevent unhealthy eating habits by making healthy food choices and sticking to them than to break the habit of unhealthy eating once you have developed a taste for junk food.

In each of these examples, it is easier to prevent bad habits from forming than to break them once they have become ingrained in your behaviour.

In Summary:

This idiom underscores the value of foresight, self-discipline, and proactive decision-making skills, to avoid detrimental consequences and the painful struggle required to break those habits later on.

#28

"Don't count your chickens before they are hatched."

The quote "Don't count your chickens before they are hatched" is a cautionary proverb often attributed to Benjamin Franklin. It is a metaphorical expression that advises against prematurely counting on or relying upon future outcomes or anticipated successes before they have actually occurred or materialised.

The meaning behind the quote is that one should avoid making assumptions about the future based solely on expectations or predictions. It encourages a more cautious and realistic approach by suggesting that it is unwise to depend on something that has not yet happened, as there are always uncertainties and unforeseen circumstances that could prevent the expected outcome.

Here's an example to illustrate the meaning of the quote: Let's say you are a student who has applied for a scholarship to study abroad. The scholarship selection process is highly competitive, and you believe you have a good chance of being selected based on your academic achievements and extracurricular activities.

Excited about the possibility of winning the scholarship, you start making plans for your future studies abroad, including researching potential universities, looking for accommodation, and even telling your friends and family about your anticipated success.

However, despite your confidence, the scholarship committee ultimately selects another candidate, and you do not receive the scholarship. This turn of events catches you off guard, and now you find yourself in a difficult position since you had already made plans and shared your expectations with others.

In this example, "counting your chickens before they are hatched" means that you assumed you would receive the scholarship before the decision was made. It implies that you should have been more cautious and waited until the outcome was certain before making concrete plans and getting your hopes up.

In Summary:

The quote serves as a reminder to not get carried away by anticipated outcomes, but to remain grounded in reality. It advises individuals to exercise patience and prudence, acknowledging that there are always risks and uncertainties that can impact future events.

#29

"Wish not so much to live long as to live well."

This quote by Benjamin Franklin emphasises the importance of prioritising the quality of one's life rather than simply focusing on its duration or length. It suggests that it is more valuable to lead a meaningful and fulfilling life rather than merely living long.

The quote encourages individuals to shift their perspective from pursuing longevity for its own sake to seeking a life filled with purpose, joy, and personal growth. It implies that the emphasis should be on the quality of experiences, relationships, and achievements rather than solely on the quantity of years.

Here's an example to illustrate the meaning of the quote: Imagine there are two individuals, Fred and Femi, both of whom are in their senior years. Fred is primarily concerned with living as long as possible. He meticulously follows all the advice on longevity, such as maintaining a strict diet, exercising excessively, and undergoing various medical treatments to prolong his life. Despite his efforts, Fred often feels unfulfilled, lonely, and dissatisfied with his existence.

On the other hand, Femi has adopted Benjamin Franklin's perspective. Instead of fixating on longevity, Femi focuses on living a well-rounded and meaningful life. He maintains a healthy lifestyle but also spends quality time with loved ones, pursuing his passions, engaging in meaningful activities, and contributing to his community. Femi finds joy and fulfilment in his relationships and hobbies.

In this example, Fred represents an individual who is solely focused on living long, while Femi embodies the philosophy of living well. The quote suggests that Femi's approach is more beneficial and rewarding, as he derives satisfaction and happiness from the richness of his experiences rather than solely from the length of his life.

In Summary:

The quote reminds us to consider the quality and purpose of our existence, rather than being solely preoccupied with extending our lifespan. It encourages us to prioritise our well-being, personal growth, and meaningful connections, as these factors contribute to a more fulfilling and satisfying life.

"Wink at small faults; when you remember that you have great ones."

This quote by Benjamin Franklin, suggests that one should be forgiving or lenient towards minor mistakes or flaws in others. Franklin advises us to overlook or ignore small faults because we know that we ourselves are not perfect, and have flaws too.

This quote emphasises the importance of understanding and compassion when dealing with the imperfections of others. Instead of harshly judging or condemning people for their minor faults, Franklin suggests adopting a more tolerant attitude.

By acknowledging our own major flaws, we become more humble and realise that we are in no position to harshly judge others for their minor slip-ups.

Here's an example to illustrate the meaning of the quote: Imagine you are a supervisor at work, and you have an employee named Joyce. Joyce is generally an excellent worker, but she occasionally arrives a few minutes late to work.

One day, she oversleeps and arrives 30 minutes late. You could react harshly and reprimand her severely for this mistake, pointing to all the previous incidents as evidence of her unprofessionalism. However, if you remember Franklin's quote, you might take a different approach.

Instead of immediately punishing her, you decide to give her the benefit of the doubt and assume that this mistake was an exception. You take her aside and gently remind her of the importance of punctuality and the impact it has on the team. By showing understanding and addressing the issue constructively rather than focusing on her minor previous faults, you give her the opportunity to rectify her behaviour and improve.

In Summary:

"Winking at small faults" means not dwelling on or magnifying minor mistakes, but instead choosing to focus on the bigger picture. It allows for a more forgiving and compassionate approach, recognising that everyone has their own shortcomings.

Chapter 6

How Rich?

#31

"Hide not your talents, they for use were made. What's a sundial in the shade?"

This quote urges us not to conceal or waste our talents and abilities. Franklin suggests that talents exist to be utilised and shared with others, and failing to do so is like setting up a sundial in a dark room. It's hidden from the sun's light and has become useless.

Each person possesses unique abilities, skills, and strengths that have the potential to make a positive impact on the world. When we hide these talents, we deprive ourselves and others of the benefits and contributions that could arise from utilising them.

The second part of the quote uses the metaphor of a sundial in the shade to illustrate the point. A sundial is a device that uses the sun's position to tell the time accurately. However, when placed in the shade, it loses its purpose and usefulness. Similarly, when talents are hidden or not put to use, they become ineffective and fail to serve their intended purpose.

Here's an example to illustrate the meaning of the quote: Imagine a person named Melody who has a remarkable talent for playing the piano. She possesses a natural gift for creating beautiful melodies and evoking emotions through her music. However, due to a lack of confidence or fear of judgment, Melody rarely shares her talent with others. She keeps her piano playing restricted to her bedroom, rarely performing for friends or participating in musical events.

In this scenario, Melody's talent remains hidden, preventing her from experiencing personal growth and potential opportunities. Furthermore, her talent goes unrecognised and unappreciated by others who could benefit from her music and find joy in her performances. It's as if she is keeping her abilities in the shade, rendering them useless and unfulfilled.

Franklin's quote encourages individuals like Melody to overcome their fears and insecurities, and to share their talents with the world. By doing so, they can make a positive impact, inspire others, and find personal fulfilment in the process. Just as a sundial relies on sunlight to serve its purpose, talents are meant to be exposed and utilised to benefit others.

In Summary:

The quote serves as a reminder to embrace and nurture one's talents, not only for personal growth but also to contribute to the greater good. It encourages individuals to have the courage to showcase their abilities, share their unique gifts, and make a positive impact on the world around them.

#32

"Do good to your friends to keep them, to your enemies to win them."

This quote suggests that one should not only show kindness and goodwill to friends in order to maintain those relationships, but also extend the same gestures to enemies as a means of potentially reconciling or winning them over.

In the first part of the quote, Franklin advises that doing good to your friends is important to maintain and strengthen those relationships. Friends are typically individuals who have shown support, loyalty, and care, and by reciprocating these positive actions, the bond between friends can be nurtured and strengthened.

However, Franklin goes beyond that and suggests that extending kindness to enemies is equally important. By doing good to your enemies, by showing them kindness, understanding, and even forgiveness—there is a possibility of transforming the relationship from one of animosity or conflict to one of mutual respect or even friendship.

Here's an example to illustrate the meaning of the quote: Imagine two colleagues, Sarah and Efrem, who have had a strained relationship in the workplace. They often disagree on projects, and their interactions are marked by tension and competitiveness. Sarah considers Efrem her enemy due to their conflicting interests and past disagreements.

Instead of harbouring resentment and continuing the cycle of animosity, Sarah decides to take Franklin's advice to heart. She realises that by doing good to her enemy, she may have an opportunity to change the dynamic between them.

Sarah approaches Efrem with a genuine desire to resolve their conflicts and improve their working relationship. She actively listens to his ideas, acknowledges his contributions, and seeks areas of common ground. Sarah offers her assistance when Efrem faces challenges and shows understanding even when they disagree. By treating Efrem with kindness and respect, Sarah aims to win him over as an ally rather than perpetuating the hostility.

In this example, Franklin's quote encourages individuals to go beyond their comfort zones and extend goodwill to those they may perceive as enemies or adversaries. By doing so, they open up the possibility of building bridges, finding common ground, and potentially transforming those relationships into more positive and productive ones.

In Summary:

This approach does not guarantee a complete transformation of an enemy into a friend, as it depends on various other factors. However, Franklin's advice encourages individuals to adopt a mindset of empathy, compassion, and understanding, with the hope of fostering positive change.

#33

"Instead of cursing the darkness, light a candle."

The quote "Instead of cursing the darkness, light a candle" by Benjamin Franklin conveys a powerful message about taking proactive and constructive action in the face of challenges or problems. Rather than complaining or being pessimistic about difficult situations, the quote encourages us to be proactive and initiate positive change.

Metaphorically, "cursing the darkness" represents being consumed by negativity, dwelling on problems, or simply complaining about the existing issues. On the other hand, "lighting a candle" symbolises taking positive steps to bring about solutions, improvements, or hope in difficult circumstances.

For example: Let's say you work in a community that is struggling with a high rate of youth unemployment and subsequent social issues. "Cursing the darkness" in this scenario would involve constantly complaining about the lack of opportunities, blaming external factors, and feeling helpless in the face of the problem.

However, applying the wisdom of Franklin's quote, "lighting a candle" would mean taking proactive steps to address the issue. You might choose to start or support a local job training program to equip young people with the necessary skills for employment. You could collaborate with local businesses to create job placement opportunities for those who complete the training.

By doing so, you actively contribute to the community's well-being and offer a potential solution to the problem of youth unemployment. In a broader sense, this quote reminds us that we have the power to make a positive impact, no matter how challenging the circumstances may be.

In Summary:

This quote encourages us to focus on solutions, take action, and try to be agents of positive change, instead of being overwhelmed by negativity or unfavourable situations. By "lighting a candle," we can inspire hope, create progress, and improve the world around us.

#34

"A place for everything, everything in its place."

This quote by Benjamin Franklin, essentially means that each item or object should have a designated spot or location where it belongs. When things are organised and kept in their proper places, it becomes easier to find them when needed and maintain order and efficiency.

This principle promotes tidiness, discipline, and an organised approach to managing one's belongings and space. It emphasises the importance of avoiding clutter and chaos, as well as the time wasted searching for misplaced items.

For example: Let's say you have a busy morning routine before leaving for work. You need to pack your bag with all the necessary items, including your wallet, keys, smartphone, and some documents. If you follow Benjamin Franklin's advice, you would have a designated spot for each of these items:

1. **Wallet:** You always keep your wallet in the top drawer of your bedside table.

2. **Keys:** You have a key hanger near the entrance door where you hang your keys every time you come home.

3. **Smartphone:** You place your smartphone on the charging station on your desk every night, so it's fully charged and ready to go in the morning.

4. **Documents:** You keep important documents in a specific folder inside your briefcase.

By following the principle of "A place for everything, everything in its place," you can quickly and easily gather all your essentials in the morning. There's no frantic search for your wallet or keys because you know exactly where to find them. This organised approach saves you time and reduces stress, allowing you to start your day on a positive note.

Additionally, this principle can be applied to other aspects of life, such as organising digital files on your computer, arranging kitchen items, or managing your workspace.

In Summary:

Overall, it encourages a systematic and disciplined approach to maintain order and efficiency in various areas of life.

#35

"Love your enemies, for they tell you your faults."

This quote suggests an unconventional perspective on how to approach those who may oppose or dislike us. Instead of harbouring resentment or animosity towards our enemies, the quote encourages us to view them as valuable sources of feedback and self-awareness.

When people who don't seem to like us criticise or point out our faults, they may be providing us with insights into areas of personal weakness. This quote advocates for a mindset of self-reflection. It also encourages us to see criticism as an opportunity for personal development rather than taking it personally.

For example: Let's say you are a manager at a company, and you have a colleague, Joshua, who constantly disagrees with your ideas and criticises your decisions during team meetings. Naturally, you find it difficult to work with him. If you follow Benjamin Franklin's advice to, "Love your enemies, for they tell you your faults"—you would take a step back and try to understand why Joshua disagrees with you.

Upon reflection, you might realise that Joshua's criticisms are centred on issues of communication. Perhaps you tend to dominate discussions and don't actively listen to other people's opinions. By taking his feedback seriously, you recognise that you need to work on your communication skills and create a more inclusive environment where team members feel their ideas are valued.

In this example, Joshua's criticism and valuable feedback, has led to personal growth and an improvement in the team dynamics. Instead of holding on to negative feelings towards Joshua, the focus was shifted to self-improvement, allowing for a positive outcome in both your personal and professional life.

In Summary:

The quote encourages us to see criticism as an opportunity for self-improvement and to approach our enemies with empathy and understanding, recognising that their feedback can help us become better versions of ourselves.

#36

"What's more valuable than Gold? Diamonds. What's more valuable than Diamonds? Virtue!"

This quote by Benjamin Franklin, is a reflection on the hierarchy of value and suggests that while gold and diamonds may be highly prized and valuable in a material sense, they are surpassed in worth by the virtue or the moral goodness of an individual.

Franklin's quote implies that material possessions, such as gold, gem stones and diamonds, are significant and are often considered valuable. Nevertheless, there is something even more precious and valuable than these material riches, namely virtue. Virtue refers to qualities of moral excellence, integrity, and ethical behaviour.

By placing virtue above wealth and material possessions, Franklin underscores the importance of character and moral values in comparison to worldly goods.

Here's an example to illustrate the meaning of the quote: Imagine two individuals, John and Robert, who are both wealthy but differ in their approach to life. John has amassed great wealth through questionable means, engaging in unethical practices and exploiting others for personal gain. He possesses vast amounts of gold and diamonds but lacks moral integrity. On the other hand, Robert leads a modest life, but he is known for his kindness, honesty, and generosity. He is respected for his virtuous character.

In this example, John's material wealth may be impressive and enviable, however, his lack of virtue diminishes the true value of his possessions. Meanwhile, Robert's virtue shines through, making him a highly regarded individual despite having fewer material riches.

Franklin's quote encourages us to prioritise and value virtue above material wealth. It reminds us that possessions alone do not define our worth or contribute to our long-term happiness. Instead, cultivating virtuous qualities and living a morally upright life brings intrinsic value, personal fulfilment, and positive impacts on others.

In Summary:

By embracing the message of this quote, we can strive to develop and embody virtues such as honesty, compassion, integrity, and empathy—recognising that these qualities are far more valuable and enduring than any material possessions we may acquire.

#37

"It is the working man who is the happy man."

This quote by Benjamin Franklin suggests that those who are engaged in productive work or meaningful labor are more likely to experience happiness and fulfilment in life —than those who don't. It highlights the importance of having purposeful employment and being industrious as a pathway to contentment and well-being.

The underlying idea is that work provides individuals with a sense of purpose, a sense of accomplishment, and a way to contribute to society.

Let's consider two individuals, Alex and Tunde:

Alex is a dedicated software developer who is passionate about creating innovative applications. He works for a tech company that values his skills and encourages him to be creative in his projects. Alex enjoys his work as he feels that he is contributing to the advancement of technology and making people's lives easier. He finds great satisfaction in overcoming coding challenges and witnessing his creations come to life. Despite facing occasional work-related stress, overall, Alex feels fulfilled and happy in his career.

On the other hand, Tunde works in a job he dislikes, merely to pay the bills. His work does not align with his interests or skills, and he often feels unappreciated and undervalued. He finds his daily tasks monotonous and lacks a sense of purpose in his role. His discontentment with his job spills over into other areas of his life, and affects his overall happiness and well-being.

In this example, Alex is the working man, and he is the happy man too. On the other hand, Tunde's unhappiness stems from his poor attitude and the lack of satisfaction and purpose feels on his job. The quote encourages us to seek out work that aligns with our passions, interests, and skills, as doing so can only lead to greater happiness and overall well-being.

In Summary:

When people are engaged in work they find fulfilling and meaningful, they are more likely to experience a sense of accomplishment and contentment in their lives. A sense of purpose and progress contributes to overall happiness.

38

"The Constitution only gives people the right to pursue happiness. You have to catch it yourself."

This quote conveys the idea that while the Constitution of a Country (e.g. The United States Constitution) guarantees its citizens the freedom and opportunity to seek happiness, it is ultimately up to each individual to take action and make choices that lead to their own happiness. In other words, the government can provide the framework and protection for the pursuit of happiness, but the responsibility for achieving happiness lies with the individual.

This quote emphasises self-determination and the idea that happiness is not simply handed to someone but is something that must be actively pursued and attained through one's own efforts and decisions. For example: Let's consider the lives of two individuals, Sarah and Michael:

Sarah lives in a country with a constitution that protects her rights and freedoms. She has access to education, job opportunities, and the freedom to make choices about her life. Sarah takes full advantage of these opportunities and works hard to pursue her passion for art. She studies art in college, puts in hours of practice, and eventually establishes herself as a successful artist. Sarah finds fulfilment and happiness in doing what she loves and achieving her goals.

Michael also lives in the same country with the same constitutional rights and freedoms as Sarah. However, he struggles to find happiness because he is indecisive and lacks motivation and direction in life. He has access to education and job opportunities but hasn't been able to commit to a career path that truly resonates with him. Michael often blames external circumstances for his unhappiness, but doesn't put in the effort needed to succeed.

In this example, the quote "The Constitution only gives people the right to pursue happiness. You have to catch it yourself" becomes evident in Sarah's experience. She seized the opportunities available to her and took initiative to pursue her passion. On the other hand, Michael's unhappiness stems from his inability to make choices and actively pursue his goals.

In Summary:

The quote reminds us that while external factors and the constitution can provide a conducive environment for the pursuit of happiness, it is ultimately our responsibility to seize opportunities, make choices, and take action to find and catch our own happiness. Happiness is not guaranteed, but through personal effort and determination, we can create a life that aligns with our values and aspirations, leading to a more fulfilling and happy existence.

39

"A good conscience is a continual Christmas."

This quote means that possessing a clear conscience, free from guilt and remorse, can bring a sense of joy and contentment that is akin to the happiness experienced during the festive and celebratory atmosphere of Christmas. It suggests that living with integrity and behaving ethically can lead to a constant state of inner peace and happiness.

In the context of people's behaviour, the quote emphasises the importance of acting in accordance with one's moral principles and values. When we consistently make decisions that align with our sense of right and wrong, we cultivate a good conscience. This can have several implications for the way we behave.

For example:

1. **Honesty:** People with a good conscience prioritise honesty and truthfulness in their actions and interactions. They are transparent in their dealings and avoid deceitful behaviour, leading to trust and respect from others.

2. **Taking Responsibility:** People with a good conscience take responsibility for their actions. If they make mistakes, they acknowledge them, seek to make amends, and learn from their experiences.

3. **Ethical Decision-making:** Integrity guides their decision-making process. They are less likely to

compromise their principles or engage in unethical practices, even when it might lead to personal gain.

4. **Peace of Mind:** Living with integrity provides a sense of peace and contentment. Knowing that their actions are in line with their values, they don't carry the burden of guilt or remorse, contributing to a happier and more fulfilling life.

5. **Positive Influence:** Individuals with a good conscience can inspire and positively influence others. Their principled behaviour sets an example for those around them, fostering a culture of integrity and moral excellence.

In Summary:

By practicing integrity and prioritising ethical behaviour, we can create an environment of trust, respect, and happiness. This not only benefits our well-being, but positively impacts the people we interact with on a daily bases. Ultimately, living with a good conscience aligns with the idea that personal integrity is the foundation of a fulfilling and meaningful life.

#40

"I never knew a man who was good at making excuses who was good at anything else."

This quote by Benjamin Franklin, conveys the idea that individuals who excel at making excuses to justify their failures or shortcomings tend to lack the ability to excel in other areas of their lives. In other words, those who frequently resort to making excuses for their actions or lack of progress are often not successful or accomplished in any other endeavour.

The quote highlights the negative impact of making excuses. Instead of taking responsibility for their actions and working to overcome challenges, such individuals often find reasons to justify their failures, which can be a self-defeating and unproductive mindset.

For example: Let's consider two individuals, Alex and Alfredo:

Alex is a driven and ambitious professional. He sets clear goals for himself and works diligently to achieve them. When faced with obstacles or failures, Alex takes ownership of his actions and mistakes. He evaluates what went wrong, learns from the experience, and adapts his approach accordingly. Rather than making excuses, Alex seeks solutions and perseveres through challenges. As a result, he makes steady progress in his career and gains the respect and trust of his colleagues and superiors.

Alfredo is also ambitious but tends to struggle when things don't go as planned. Instead of taking responsibility for his actions, he frequently makes excuses to justify his failures or missed deadlines. He blames external factors, colleagues, or circumstances for his lack of success. As a result, Alfredo's reputation in the workplace suffers, and he finds it challenging to make significant progress in his career.

His tendency to make excuses becomes a barrier to personal growth and improvement. Colleagues and superiors perceive him as unreliable and lacking accountability. This leads to missed opportunities for advancement, promotion or recognition.

In this example, the quote by Benjamin Franklin becomes evident through the experiences of Alex and Alfredo. Alex's ability to take responsibility for his actions and avoid making excuses enables him to learn from his mistakes and continuously improve. On the other hand, Alfredo's habit of making excuses hinders his personal and professional development, preventing him from reaching his full potential.

In Summary:

The quote serves as a valuable reminder of the importance of personal accountability and the negative consequences of consistently making excuses. Excuses can create a pattern of avoiding challenges and personal growth, whereas accepting responsibility and learning from setbacks can lead to greater resilience and self-improvement. By adopting a proactive and responsible mindset, we can overcome obstacles, make progress, and achieve our goals more effectively.

Chapter 7

How Tragic?

#41

"Life's tragedy is that we get old too soon and wise too late."

This quote by Benjamin Franklin conveys a poignant truth about the passage of time and the nature of wisdom. It suggests that as we go through life, we often gain wisdom and understanding through experience, but by the time we have accumulated this wisdom, we may find ourselves at an older age, with limited time left to fully apply or benefit from the insights we have gained.

Let's consider the experience of a middle-aged man called Mike. Mike is a middle-aged individual who has been through various ups and downs in his personal and professional life. Over the years, he has accumulated a wealth of experiences and insights. As he looks back on his journey, he recognises that many of the important life lessons he has learned came later in life.

He realises that he would have made different choices and decisions if he had possessed the wisdom he has now, during his younger years. While he can still use his wisdom to guide his future decisions, he can't turn back time to fully benefit from the knowledge he has gained.

In this example, Mike's experience illustrates the realisation that wisdom often arrives later in life when there may be fewer opportunities to apply it to the fullest extent.

In Summary:

The quote serves as a reminder to value and seek wisdom at every stage of life and to learn from the experiences of others who may have walked similar paths before us. It also underscores the importance of being receptive to advice and guidance, especially if we are young, as the insights of others can save us from unnecessary hardships and regrets in the long run.

#42

"Without continual growth and progress, such words as improvement, achievement, and success have no meaning."

This quote by Benjamin Franklin, conveys the idea that the concepts of improvement, achievement, and success are inherently linked to ongoing development and forward movement. In other words, to truly understand and appreciate the significance of improvement, achievement, and success, one must be in a state of continuous growth and progress.

It highlights the importance of embracing a growth mindset and consistently striving to better oneself, as it is through this process of continual improvement that accomplishments and success gain true significance and value.

For example: Let's consider the journey of two individuals:

Lisa is a highly motivated individual who is always seeking opportunities for personal and professional growth. She sets ambitious goals for herself and actively seeks ways to enhance her skills and knowledge. Lisa regularly attends workshops, takes online courses, and seeks feedback from mentors to refine her abilities. Over time, her dedication to continual growth results in significant improvements in her performance and a strong sense of achievement. When Lisa accomplishes her goals and achieves success, she understands the true value of her accomplishments because they are the result of her ongoing efforts to progress and improve.

James, on the other hand, is resistant to change and tends to stay within his comfort zone. He is content with his current skill set and rarely seeks opportunities for growth. James avoids challenges and prefers to stick to familiar routines. As a result, he experiences limited personal and professional development. While James may achieve some success based on his existing abilities, he may not fully appreciate the value of his achievements because they do not reflect a journey of continual growth and progress.

Lisa's dedication to ongoing growth gives her accomplishments and success a deeper significance and fulfilment, as they are the outcomes of her constant pursuit of improvement. In contrast, James may achieve certain milestones, but without embracing continual growth, he may not fully maximise his potential.

In Summary:

The quote serves as a reminder of the importance of embracing a growth mindset, seeking opportunities to learn and develop, and consistently striving to progress in life. By doing so, improvement, achievement, and success take on profound meaning and become a reflection of our journey of continual growth and self-improvement.

#43

"Well done is better than well said."

The quote by Benjamin Franklin conveys the idea that actions and results speak louder, and hold more value than mere words or promises. It emphasises the importance of taking tangible actions and achieving real outcomes rather than just talking about what one intends to do. In essence, it suggests that accomplishments and deeds carry more weight and credibility, than empty promises or eloquent speeches.

For example: Consider two individuals, Yemi and James, who are both tasked with leading a charity fundraising campaign:

Yemi is known for her persuasive and charismatic communication skills. She excels at delivering inspiring speeches, motivating others, and sharing grand plans for the charity campaign. However, when it comes to the actual execution of the campaign, Yemi falls short. She struggles to translate her words into meaningful actions. Despite her convincing speeches, the fundraising results are disappointing, as she fails to effectively implement the strategies she talked about.

James, on the other hand, is not as articulate as Yemi when it comes to speaking. However, he is a person of action. He may not deliver the most eloquent speeches, but he focuses on planning, organising, and executing the charity campaign effectively. James works closely with his team, sets achievable goals, and ensures that every step of the campaign is well-implemented. As a result, the fundraising efforts under James' leadership are successful, and the campaign achieves its targets.

In this example, the quote "Well done is better than well said" is apparent. Despite Yemi's persuasive speeches and promises, her lack of tangible results undermines the impact of her words. On the other hand, James' focus on actual execution and achievement of results gives greater weight and value to his efforts, even though his communication may not be as captivating as Yemi's.

In Summary:

This quote serves as a valuable reminder of the importance of backing up words with actions and delivering tangible results. In various aspects of life, whether it's in leadership, relationships, or personal endeavours, demonstrating concrete accomplishments and achievements carries more significance and earns greater trust and respect, than empty talk or promises.

#44

"Keep your eyes wide open before marriage and half shut afterward."

This quote by Benjamin Franklin, offers a piece of advice regarding the perspective one should adopt before and after getting married.

"Keep your eyes wide open before marriage" suggests that before entering into a marital commitment, one should be observant, attentive, and fully aware of their partner's characteristics, values, and flaws. It advises individuals to make an informed decision by thoroughly understanding their potential spouse's personality, habits, and compatibility with their own. That's why it's not wise to get married before you've had plenty of time to know your spouse.

"Half shut afterward" implies that after the marriage, there should be a willingness to overlook or accept certain imperfections or minor shortcomings in your partner. It signifies a level of tolerance and understanding, focusing on the positive aspects of the relationship and avoiding unnecessary nitpicking or overcritical behaviour.

The quote reminds us that while it's essential to be discerning and thoughtful before entering into a lifelong commitment, it's equally crucial to adopt a more forgiving and compassionate attitude once married. Why? Because you recognise that no one is perfect and that successful relationships often require some level of compromise and tolerance.

In Summary:

Franklin advises us to be vigilant and observant in choosing a life partner but forgiving and understanding once married.

#45

"The doors of wisdom are never shut."

This quote by Benjamin Franklin, conveys the idea that learning and gaining knowledge have no boundaries or limits. It suggests that there is always something new to learn and discover, regardless of one's age, experiences, or achievements. Wisdom is not a destination but a continuous journey of growth and enlightenment.

The quote emphasises that the pursuit of wisdom and knowledge is an ongoing process that does not end. No matter how much knowledge one may possess, there is always room for more learning and understanding. It encourages individuals to remain open-minded, curious, and receptive to new ideas and experiences. The quote also suggests that one should approach life with humility, recognising that they do not have all the answers and that there is always room for improvement.

Let's consider an example of a renowned scientist, who has made significant contributions to his field of study over the years. Dr. Smith has earned various accolades and is widely regarded as an expert in his domain. However, despite his achievements and recognition, Dr. Smith firmly believes in Benjamin Franklin's quote.

So, he attends international conferences, where other researchers present their latest findings. Instead of dismissing these presentations as irrelevant or insignificant, Dr. Smith actively engages with the new information and research. He asks questions, seeks clarifications, and expresses genuine interest in the work of his peers.

After the conference, Dr. Smith spends time reflecting on the new insights gained during the event. He realises that there are novel approaches and methodologies that he had not considered before. This realisation prompts him to embark on new research collaborations and explore different avenues of inquiry.

In this example, Dr. Smith exemplifies the spirit of continuous learning and the openness to embrace new ideas, despite his already established status in the scientific community.

In Summary:

The quote encourages individuals like Dr. Smith to remain humble, receptive, and eager to keep their minds open to further wisdom and growth. It is a reminder that no matter how much one knows or has accomplished, there is always more to learn and discover. In short, learning is a lifelong journey.

#46

"Content makes poor men rich; discontentment makes rich men poor."

This quote by Benjamin Franklin, carries a profound message about the impact of one's mindset and attitude on their sense of wealth and well-being.

The first part of the quote, "Content makes poor men rich," suggests that true richness or wealth is not merely measured by material possessions or financial status. Instead, contentment with what one has can lead to a sense of fulfilment, even in situations of limited resources.

The second part of the quote, "Discontentment makes rich men poor," highlights that no matter how much material wealth someone may possess, if they are constantly discontent and unsatisfied, they can experience a form of poverty and unhappiness in their mind and attitude.

For example: Let's consider two individuals to illustrate this quote:

Raj comes from a modest background. He has a small house, a stable job that pays enough to cover his basic needs, and a loving family. Raj is content with his life. He values the time spent with his family, finds joy in simple pleasures, and appreciates the security and stability that his job provides. Despite not having excessive wealth or luxury, Raj considers himself rich because he is happy and content with what he has.

Josh, on the other hand, is a wealthy businessman with numerous properties, luxury cars, and a successful business empire. Despite his immense wealth, he is always discontent. He is constantly striving for more profits, a bigger mansion, and more recognition. However, no matter how successful Josh becomes, he is never truly satisfied. His insatiable desire for more keeps him in a perpetual state of discontentment, making him feel poor despite his wealth.

In this example, Raj represents the first part of the quote, and Josh exemplifies the second part of the quote.

In Summary:

The quote encourages individuals to find contentment and satisfaction in their present circumstances and not to equate wealth solely with material possessions. It reminds us that true richness comes from appreciating what we have and being content with it, while discontentment can lead to a sense of poverty, even in the presence of great wealth.

47

"Be at war with your vices, at peace with your neighbours, and let every new year find you a better person."

This quote by Benjamin Franklin, "Be at war with your vices, at peace with your neighbours, and let every new year find you a better person," provides valuable life advice in three distinct aspects of personal development.

Firstly, "Be at War with Your Vices".

This part of the quote suggests that individuals should actively confront and challenge their vices, weaknesses, or negative habits. It encourages self-awareness and the willingness to improve oneself by recognising and addressing personal shortcomings.

Secondly, "Be at Peace with Your Neighbours".

Here, "neighbours" not only refers to those living nearby but also all with whom one interacts in society. This part of the quote advocates for harmonious relationships and emphasises the importance of cooperation, understanding, and empathy towards others.

Thirdly, "Let Every New Year Find You a Better Person".

This part highlights the continuous nature of self-improvement. It encourages individuals to set goals, learn from past experiences, and strive for personal growth and development throughout their lives.

Let's see how Emma embodies the message of this quote:

Emma is a middle-aged woman who has struggled with anger issues for much of her life. She tends to get easily frustrated and loses her temper in various situations. At the beginning of the year, Emma reflects on her behaviour and acknowledges her problem with anger. She decides to deal a deadly blow to this vice and take active steps to address it.

Throughout the year, Emma attends anger management classes, practices mindfulness techniques, and seeks council to understand the root causes of her anger. She also learns healthier ways to cope with stress and difficult emotions. By making a conscious effort and being persistent in her endeavours, Emma gradually becomes better at managing her anger.

In terms of being at peace with her neighbours, Emma takes the initiative to resolve conflicts and misunderstandings with her co-workers and family members. She learns to communicate more effectively and empathetically, which leads to improved relationships.

As the year comes to a close, Emma reflects on her journey of self-improvement. She realises that she has indeed become a better person compared to the start of the year. She is now more in control of her anger, has healthier relationships, and feels a sense of accomplishment in her personal growth.

In this example, Emma embodies the wisdom of the quote. She waged a personal battle against her vices, worked towards harmonious relationships with others, and allowed every new year to mark a continuous journey of self-improvement.

In Summary:

Franklin encourages us to actively combat our vices and faults, maintain harmonious relationships with others, and strive for continuous personal growth and improvement.

#48

"Little minds think and talk about people. Average minds think and talk about actions and things. Great minds think and talk about ideas."

This quote highlights the different levels of thinking and conversation that people engage in, ranging from the superficial to the profound.

Level 1... People with "little minds" tend to focus their thoughts and conversations on gossip, rumours, and personal judgments about others. They may be preoccupied with discussing people's lives, appearance, and behaviour, often in a negative or judgmental manner.

Level 2... Individuals with "average minds" tend to discuss actions and material things. They may talk about daily events, activities, or possessions. Their conversations may revolve around mundane topics, such as the weather, sports, or possessions.

Level 3... "Great minds" are those who engage in deep and insightful thinking. They ponder and discuss abstract concepts, principles, and ideas. Their conversations delve into the realms of philosophy, science, art, and other profound subjects.

Challenge: What do you preoccupy yourself with, when you converse with friends, colleagues or family members? If you are not sure, make a note of all your discussions and conversations with people over the next 21 days. Hopefully, the exercise will help you understand what kind of mind you have developed—based on Franklin's quote.

In Summary:

The quote encourages individuals to aspire to develop their thinking beyond the surface level of people and actions. It inspires people to cultivate their intellectual curiosity and engage in conversations that lead to personal and spiritual growth; and a deeper understanding of themselves and the world the live in.

#49

"The heart of a fool is in his mouth, but the mouth of a wise man is in his heart."

This quote by Benjamin Franklin, contrasts the way fools and wise individuals speak and express themselves:

1. **The Heart of a Fool is in His Mouth:** This part of the quote suggests that foolish people tend to speak

94

impulsively without much thought. Their words are often driven by their emotions and lack of consideration, leading to hasty or thoughtless remarks.

2. **The Mouth of a Wise Man is in His Heart:** On the other hand, this part of the quote indicates that wise individuals carefully consider their words before speaking. They speak from a place of thoughtfulness and wisdom, ensuring that their words are well-chosen and aligned with their intentions and values.

Let's consider two colleagues, Bob and Michael, to illustrate how this quote can be applied in their interactions:

Scenario 1 - Bob (Foolish):

Bob and Michael are working on a team project. During a heated discussion about a particular approach to the project, Bob becomes frustrated with Michael's ideas. Instead of calmly expressing his concerns, Bob lets his emotions take over. He raises his voice, makes personal attacks on Michael's abilities, and dismisses his ideas without giving them proper consideration. Bob's words are rash and thoughtless, causing tension and resentment within the team.

Scenario 2 - Michael (Wise):

In another situation, Michael finds himself in a disagreement with a colleague over a different matter. He takes a moment to compose his thoughts and carefully considers the best way to express his concerns. When the time is right, Michael calmly addresses the issue, using respectful language and constructive feedback. He explains his perspective and is open to understanding his colleague's point of view. Michael's words carry wisdom and empathy, fostering a positive and productive conversation.

In these examples, Bob's behaviour represents the "heart of a fool is in his mouth" part of the quote. He allows his emotions to dictate his words, leading to negative consequences for both himself and others. On the other hand, Michael exemplifies the "mouth of a wise man is in his heart" part of the quote. He demonstrates the ability to control his emotions, consider the impact of his words, and communicate thoughtfully and respectfully.

In Summary:

The quote serves as a reminder to be mindful of our words and to speak from a place of wisdom and empathy. It encourages us to think before we speak, considering the consequences of our words and choosing them carefully. By doing so, we can foster better communication and build stronger relationships.

#50

"The doorstep to the temple of wisdom is a knowledge of our own ignorance."

This quote by Benjamin Franklin, highlights the importance of humility and self-awareness in the pursuit of knowledge and wisdom. The quote suggests that to gain true wisdom, one must first acknowledge their own ignorance or lack of knowledge. Being humble and recognising that there is much to learn opens the door to enlightenment and understanding.

Understanding one's own limitations and areas of ignorance allows one to seek knowledge actively. By acknowledging what we don't know, we become more receptive to learning and growth.

Let's consider an example to illustrate this quote:

Sarah is a recent college graduate who has just started her career as a junior software developer. She is excited about her new job but also feels a bit overwhelmed by the complex coding tasks and projects she is assigned.

Case 1: Ignorance of Ignorance.

In this scenario, Sarah believes she knows everything there is to know about software development, given her recent graduation with honours. She dismisses the advice of her more experienced colleagues, assuming that she is already well-versed in all aspects of her job. Due to her overconfidence and lack of humility, she doesn't seek additional guidance or learn from others. As a result, she makes many mistakes in her work, and her performance suffers.

Case 2 - Knowledge of Ignorance.

In this scenario, Sarah acknowledges that despite her education, she is still relatively new to the industry. She understands that she has much to learn from her experienced colleagues and the challenges presented in her projects. With humility and self-awareness, she actively seeks out guidance and advice from her team members. She asks questions, attends workshops, and pursues online courses to improve her skills.

In this example, Case 2 embodies the essence of Benjamin Franklin's quote. Sarah's awareness of her own ignorance about certain aspects of software development motivates her to seek knowledge actively. By being humble and open to learning, she gains access to the temple of wisdom, gradually becoming more skilled and proficient in her profession.

In Summary:

Franklin highlights that true wisdom begins with recognising one's own lack of knowledge and understanding. Self-awareness of our ignorance opens the door to seeking knowledge and wisdom.

Benjamin Franklin's Global Impact

For over 230 years, Benjamin Franklin's influence has left a lasting impact on millions of people around the world. As a statesman, inventor and philosopher, Franklin's ideas and principles have transcended time and cultural boundaries, resonating with individuals from all sorts of backgrounds.

One aspect of Franklin's influence lies in his emphasis on the value of education and knowledge. His belief in the power of continuous learning has inspired countless individuals to prioritise education as a pathway to personal growth and empowerment. This dedication to self-improvement has motivated people to seek opportunities for learning and development; resulting in a more knowledgeable and informed society.

Another significant contribution is Franklin's advocacy for discipline and balanced living. By promoting the importance of a healthy lifestyle and time management, he has encouraged individuals to lead well-regulated lives, fostering physical and mental well-being. His emphasis on self-care and punctuality has been embraced by millions seeking to enhance their overall quality of life.

Franklin's resilience and determination have also been a source of inspiration for many. His example of overcoming challenges and obstacles has encouraged individuals to persevere in the face of adversity. This philosophy of persistence has become a driving force for those pursuing their goals and aspirations, leading to greater achievements and personal growth.

Finally, Franklin's insights into the significance of diplomacy and peaceful resolutions have had a profound impact on international relations. His understanding of the devastating consequences of conflict has influenced policymakers and peace advocates to prioritise dialogue and diplomatic solutions over violence and war.

In conclusion, Benjamin Franklin's influence extends to millions of people worldwide, impacting various aspects of their lives. From the pursuit of knowledge and wisdom to fostering discipline, resilience, and peace, Franklin's words have left a profound impact on the lives of individuals from diverse walks of life. His timeless wisdom continues to inspire, motivate, and guide people across generations, making him an influential figure whose ideas remain as relevant today as they were centuries ago.

More Fascinating Quotes by Benjamin Franklin

- Would you live with ease, do what you ought and not what you please?

- Speak ill of no man, but speak all the good you know of everybody.

- If a man empties his purse into his head, no man can take it away from him.

- The faithful see the invisible, believe the incredible and then receive the impossible.

- If everyone is thinking alike, then no one is really thinking.

- A slip of the foot you may soon recover, but a slip of the tongue you may never get over.

- The heart of a fool is in his mouth, but the mouth of a wise man is in his heart.

- He that is good for making excuses is seldom good for anything else.

- We are all born ignorant, but one must work hard to remain stupid.

- Dost thou love life? Then do not squander time; for that's the stuff life is made of.

- A brother may not be a friend, but a friend will always be a brother.

- The best thing to give to your enemy is forgiveness; to an opponent, tolerance; to a friend, your heart; to your child, a good example; to yourself, respect; to all others, charity.

- I am for doing good to the poor, but I think the best way of doing good to the poor, is not making them at ease in poverty, but leading or driving them out of it.

- To be content, look backward on those who possess less than yourself, not forward on those who possess more. If this does not make you content, you don't deserve to be happy.

- Remember not only to say the right thing in the right place, but far more difficult still, to leave unsaid the wrong thing at the tempting moment.

- If you would know the value of money, go try to borrow some; for he that goes a-borrowing goes a-sorrowing.

- I didn't fail the test, I just found 100 ways to do it wrong.

- Beware of little expenses. A small leak will sink a great ship.

- He that is of the opinion money will do everything may well be suspected of doing everything for money.

- How many observe Christ's birthday! How few observe His precepts!

- Being ignorant is not so much a shame, as being unwilling to learn.

- He who sacrifices freedom for security deserves neither.

- Having been poor is no shame, being ashamed of it is.

- He that lies down with Dogs, shall rise up with fleas.

- A man of words and not of deeds, is like a garden full of weeds.

- An ounce of prevention is worth a pound of cure.

- When you're good to others, you're best to yourself.

- We must all hang together, or assuredly we shall all hang separately.

- Trouble knocked at the door, but, hearing laughter, hurried away.

- War is when the government tells you who the bad guy is. Revolution is when you decide that for yourself.

- Reading makes a full man, meditation a profound man, discourse a clear man.

- Do not anticipate trouble, or worry about what may never happen.

- If you know how to spend less than you get, you have the philosopher's stone.

- The best of all medicines are rest and fasting.

- Fear to do ill, and you need fear nothing else.

- Be studious in your profession, and you will be learned. Be industrious and frugal and you will be rich. Be sober and temperate and you will be healthy. Be in general virtuous and you will be happy.

From the Author

Thank you again for purchasing this book.
If you enjoyed reading it (and I certainly hope you did),
I would appreciate it if you would rate it fairly for me
and for the benefit of other potential readers. Please
post a short review on any of the sites that sell it.

Thank you very much!

About the Author

Dr. Tony Peters and his wife, Shola —are an inspiring couple dedicated to empowering others to embrace their faith, nurture meaningful relationships, and embrace a life of fruitfulness and abundance. 

Tony serves as the Founding Pastor of The King's House—affectionately known as London's Alive Church. His calling extends beyond the pulpit, as he also teaches in Bible Schools and equips Church leaders and their members in the areas of faith, family and finances.

With a life devoted to guiding others towards a path of faithfulness and fruitfulness, Tony invites you to embark on a journey that has the power to elevate your connection with God, enrich your relationships with others, and inspire a healthy, prosperous, and fulfilling existence.

Tony and his wife reside and pastor in the United Kingdom. They have two adult children who love God and serve in the Church and two cherished grandchildren.

Other Books by the Author

- **SURPLUS MONEY** – How to get out of Debt, build lasting Wealth and leave a legacy of Abundance

- **Secrets of a Lasting Marriage** – 7 Vital Building Blocks for a Healthy Marriage

- **How to Build a Rock Solid Marriage** – Choices That Will Give You the Marriage of Your Dreams

- **Ten Keys to Effective Communication in Marriage**

- **Stress No More** – 20 Healthy Ways To Reduce Stress, Anxiety & Worry

- **Maximising Your Season of Singleness** – Using Your Season of Singleness to Prepare for Marriage

- **Keeping God At The Centre Of Your Marriage** – Simple Ways To Keep God At The Centre Of Your Relationship

- **How to Rescue Your Marriage from Breaking Up** – Avoiding the Ten Major Relationship Killers

- **Find Your Soul Mate God's Way** – Say Goodbye To Dating

- **21 Crucial Things They Don't Teach Young People About Sex**

- **Equipping Your Children for Life** – Tools your Children should not leave Home without

- **Understand Your Marriage Vows** - What the Marriage Vows Mean and How to Honour Them

- **Why God Wants You & Your Family in a Life-giving Church** – 12 Reasons to Get Involved in a Great Local Church...

- **Why Can't We Talk About It?** – 4 Practical Steps to Help Reduce Misunderstandings During Conversations by Shola Peters

- **How to Find a Life-giving Church** – You Can Thrive in

All books are available at reputable booksellers online and in print

Or

(www.rocksolidmarriages.com)